Making Memory Boxes

there's no place like home

Making Memory Boxes

35 Beautiful Projects

Anna Corba

Sterling Publishing Co., Inc. New York
A Sterling/Chapelle Book

Chapelle, Ltd. Inc.
P.O. Box 9252, Ogden, UT 84409
(801) 621-2777 • (801) 621-2788 Fax
e-mail: chapelle@chapelleltd.com
Web site: www.chapelleltd.com

Every effort has been made to ensure that all information in this book is accurate. However, due to differing conditions, tools, and individual skills, the publisher cannot be responsible for any injuries, losses, and/or other damages which may result from the use of the information in this book.

This volume is meant to stimulate craft ideas. If readers are unfamiliar or not proficient in a skill necessary to attempt a project, we urge that they refer to an instructional book specifically addressing the required technique.

Library of Congress Cataloging-in-Publication Data available

Corba, Anna.
  Making memory boxes : 35 beautiful projects / Anna Corba.
      p. cm.
  "A Sterling Chapelle Book."
  Includes index.
  ISBN 1-4027-1532-3
1. Box making. 2. Ornamental boxes. 3. Assemblage (Art) 4. Souvenirs (Keepsakes) I. Title.
  TT870.5.C675 2005
  745.593--dc22

                                        2005008738
10 9 8 7 6 5 4 3 2
Published by Sterling Publishing Co., Inc.
387 Park Avenue South, New York, NY 10016
©2005 by Anna Corba
Distributed in Canada by Sterling Publishing
c/o Canadian Manda Group, 165 Dufferin Street
Toronto, Ontario, Canada M6K 3H6
Distributed in the United Kingdom by GMC Distribution Services,
Castle Place, 166 High Street, Lewes, East Sussex, England BN7 1XU
Distributed in Australia by Capricorn Link (Australia) Pty. Ltd.
P. O. Box 704, Windsor, NSW 2756, Australia
Printed and Bound in China
All Rights Reserved

Sterling ISBN 1-4027-1532-3

For information about custom editions, special sales, premium and corporate purchases, please contact Sterling Special Sales Department at 800-805-5489 or specialsales@sterlingpub.com.

Table of Contents

a day to celebrate

Memory Boxes

Introduction

Introduction

What Is a Memory Box?

I think of memories as our personal treasures, things that remind us who we are and connect us to where we have been. To capture a memory specifically and artistically is to honor a person or event that has touched and enriched our lives. In doing so, we also briefly relive the moment and perhaps create an object that can be kept in one's own collection or passed on to others for years to come.

I find a box to be an intriguing format in which to explore personal issues due to its endless versatility and variety. A box can be addressed from inside or out, hanging from a wall, or standing open on a shelf. It can be an art piece in itself or the base from which another idea can be explored.

I like to approach a box as a mystery waiting to be discovered. Will the untying of that beautiful velvet bow reveal letters that have been held secret for years, or merely an empty compartment awaiting new direction? Will I sit this box on a special shelf with others or peer inside its space and find potential?

All kinds of objects can be considered boxes: empty drawers, fruit baskets, utensil trays, and old film canisters all come to mind. Each is an appropriate starting point—anything that can hold contents or be a framework upon which to build a story is a box in my book.

The point of making a memory box is in the process—the exploration, the willingness to step back, take a breath and allow your creative desire to unfold. There's no telling which memories, cherished or long forgotten, may rise to the surface. Be observant and be inspired. It's your journey.

Chapter One

Basic Processes

Star Roses

Basic Processes

Tea Dye

Tea works equally well for staining paper or natural fabrics and comes in handy when you love an item that isn't quite aged enough. My rule of thumb is two tea bags per gallon of water. Simply boil water and pour over tea bags laid out in a flat pan. I use an assortment of old enamel pans I've picked up at garage sales, allowing them to stain over the years. For a light stain, let your paper steep for about an hour. For a deeper color, double the amount of tea bags as well as the steeping time. Raspberry tea will lend a pink hue to all your items, which is pretty but will also smell a bit fruity.

After the items have steeped sufficiently, drain the water and spread them on paper towels to dry overnight. Paper tends to roll up at the edges when dry. It can be flattened under heavy books once it has dried.

You also can try experimenting with coffee. Steep the coffee in a handpress and pour over the paper or fabric. Coffee delivers a deeper, browner tone than tea and also can have an aroma.

Beeswax

My favorite wax is bleached beeswax, but it is not always easy to find. University art stores are usually your best bet or it can be ordered. Unbleached beeswax, either in crystals or in blocks, can work; but it will leave a slightly yellow cast. There are times when I simply use a creamy candle wax, which is easy to find at most craft stores. I mix this one-third wax to two-thirds paraffin. Otherwise it is just too soft to hold up. Its softness is fun to manipulate, however; so if you want lots of drips and character, go ahead and use this wax.

You will need to purchase an electric skillet with sides that you don't mind ruining. I have been lucky to find these at sidewalk sales or church rummage sales. If you are using blocks of wax, cut the blocks into 2" cubes. Melt the wax to 200°F but do not heat over 200°F. Have enough to fill the skillet at least ¼" deep. It also works to melt the wax in a bread pan placed on the skillet. It takes slightly longer to melt, but it is an easy way to get a nice deep pool of wax.

Lay your box down on newsprint close to the skillet. Dip a chip brush in wax to saturate it, then quickly and evenly spread onto the box. Repeat strokes until surface is covered, overlapping the previous stroke slightly. The wax will dry quickly. I like the imperfections that occur in the surface, but if you would like a smoother look, you can achieve this by gently scraping with a razor blade.

It is fun to experiment with the wax. You can dip three-dimensional objects in it and they will be dry in a matter of moments. You can use it as an adhesive to add items to an already finished piece. Simply stroke the wax over the addition, such as a paper scrap or postage stamp, until it stays in place. I like drips to run down at this point.

When finished, simply unplug the skillet and allow the wax to cool and harden with the brush right in it. This makes for easy storage and the brush will soften back up when you reheat the wax. Scrape the bristles with a wooden craft stick to help keep them supple during the reheating process.

Most Commonly Used Tools

Clean dry cloths

Craft glue

Double-stick tape

Glue stick

Hammer/nails

Hot-glue gun/hot-glue sticks

Ink pads

Paintbrushes/sponge brushes

Pencil

Photocopier

Rubber stamp images and alphabet

Sandpaper, assorted grits

Scissors: craft, decorative-edged, fabric, pinking shears

Wire cutters

Chapter
Two
Outside
the Box

Outside the Box

These boxes serve a function, whether it's to store a special collection or house odds and ends that may otherwise go unnoticed. The idea is to make the outside of the box so enticing that it becomes imperative to peek inside.

Favorite recipes, recital programs, or even just snippets of beautiful ribbon can be organized into a wide variety of decorative containers that become keepsakes in themselves.

Culinary Comforts

Alphabet rubber stamps
Black acrylic paint
Index cards
Ink pads
Matte medium
Sprig of vintage fruit
Unfinished basic recipe box
Vegetable/fruit catalog

Fill this box with special family recipes handed down for generations, or with recipes for comfort foods that recall happy memories.

1. Paint recipe box black and allow to dry. Add a second coat. When thoroughly dry, sand edges to create a slightly aged look.

2. Rip appealing pages from catalog. Tear individual illustrations neatly yet artfully; some can be folded and creased to create a clean edge while others can be torn freehand for a more textured border.

3. Using matte medium, apply illustrations to all sides of the box, allowing some black to show through. *Note: I left the top of the recipe box blank and applied an illustration to the inside lid instead.*

4. Stamp index cards with alphabet letters most commonly used in the recipes to find things quickly.

5. Use a sprig of vintage fruit to mark your place when removing cards.

Another Idea

{ Divide the cards into categories such as morning, noon, and night; or nibbles, snacks, and meals. }

F. W. WURZBURG,

WHOLESALE AND RETAIL DEALER IN

Dry Goods, Carpets and Oil Cloths,

Laces and Embroideries,

Ladies' and Gents' Furnishing Goods,

Shawls and Silks, Dress Goods,

80 & 82 Canal Street,

GRAND RAPIDS, ▪ MICHIGAN.

FULL LINE OF "CORTICELLI" SPOOL SILK.

An Evening at the Opera

I like to have a special box for opera and ballet programs. You also can use this to keep your children's recital and school play programs.

1. Trim sheet music to cover top of photo box. Apply with matte medium and press down gently with cloth to smooth out all air bubbles.

2. Cut velvet ribbon to fit perimeter of box lid. Adhere to lid on all sides with craft glue, leaving a ¼" margin along top and bottom edges of ribbon.

3. Trim two velvet strips to width of box lid and glue in place to define top and bottom borders of sheet music.

4. Choose a title for box from old wooden scrabble pieces. Hot-glue into place.

Tip

{ You may want to color the tiles with a wood stain to achieve an aged quality. }

Black photo box

Craft glue

Hot-glue gun

Matte medium

Scrabble letters

Sheet music

Velvet ribbon

21

MARIE DE MÉDICIS

Fille du Grand Duc de Toscane François Ier, née en 1573 à Florence. En 1600 elle épousa Henri IV, mais ne put jamais s'entendre avec lui et à sa mort fut déclarée Régente. Elle donna toute sa confiance à Concini (1611), puis maria Louis XIII à Anne d'Autriche et fut toute puissante, jusqu'à l'arrivée de De Luynes au pouvoir. Elle fut exilée par lui, fut vaincue aux Ponts-de-Cé et ne traita que grâce à Richelieu. À la mort de De Luynes, elle revint à la Cour et fit entrer Richelieu au Conseil. Plus tard, voyant l'ascendant qu'il prenait sur le roi, elle voulut le faire disgrâcier; mais il vainquit l'esprit du roi à la Journée des Dupes (1630), et elle fut exilée à Compiègne, puis dut quitter la France, passa dans les Pays-Bas, en Angleterre et enfin à Cologne où elle mourut en 1642. Elle protégea les Arts. On lui doit la construction du Luxembourg.

ND Phot

Carte Postale

Tous les pays étrangers n'acceptent pas la correspondance au recto.
Se renseigner à la poste.

Correspondance
❧

Adresse
❧

Springtime Memories

This little green box was so beautiful "as is" that I only embellished slightly to make it more functional. Choose your box carefully, with a color palette you enjoy.

1. Apply title page to inside of spice box with matte medium. Smooth out with cloth. *Note: Title page will serve to keep box open.*

2. Trim velvet ribbon to wrap around box. Adhere with small dabs of craft glue at 1" intervals. Press against box gently.

3. Glue button at front center.

4. Arrange flowers within the box. *Note: You can either leave the stems loose for easy rearranging or insert into a Styrofoam form wedged into bottom of box.*

Craft glue

Matte medium

Mother-of-pearl button

Old spice box

Title page from old book

Velvet ribbon

Vintage flowers

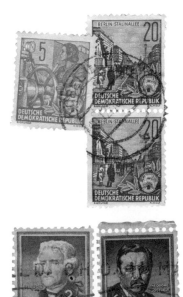

Sweet Treats

Certain treats become traditions on various holidays. I fill these boxes with chocolate kisses for Valentine's Day and chocolate eggs for Easter.

1. Paint boxes white, both inside and out. This will take two coats; allow to dry between coats.

2. Color-copy trading card if you would like to keep the original. Trim with decorative-edged scissors.

3. Using decorative paper, create background for trading card. Apply to box lid with matte medium. Adhere trading card image to center of background with craft glue, so the paper creates a colorful border. Press firmly.

4. Stamp polka dots on box lid in a random pattern. Allow some dots to extend around the edges.

5. Trim mini pom-poms to surround perimeter of box lid. Dab a dot of craft glue on fabric band above each pom-pom. Beginning at the back, firmly press trim to bottom edge of box lid, gluing one side at a time. Make certain edge line remains straight.

6. Let dry overnight.

7. Fill with chocolate kisses or other wrapped candies.

Craft glue

Decorative paper

Decorative-edged scissors

Chocolate kisses or other individually wrapped candies

Ink pads, various colors

Kraft boxes, 7½"x7½"x3"

Matte medium

Mini pom-pom trim

Polka-dot rubber stamp

Vintage trading cards

White acrylic paint

Ribbon Box

I collect ribbons from special packages and store them in their own ribbon box. I often dip inside when I need an unusual snippet.

1. Rubber-stamp image onto five 3"x5" ledger pages.

2. Adhere pages to box at 3" intervals around box lid, ¾" up from base of box.

3. Drill ten holes at 3" intervals around box lid, ½" up from bottom edge of lid.

4. Thread seam binding through front of hole, using needle. Leave left side a bit longer and tie a one-sided bow.

5. Drill two holes ½" apart from each other into center of lid's top. Pull striped ribbon up from inside of lid, using needle. Tie a generous bow.

6. Cut decorative ribbon to fit circumference of lid's top. Dab with craft glue at ½" intervals and press firmly to box lid ½" down from top.

(24") Striped wire-edged ribbon, 1½" wide

(10) 12" lengths of rayon seam binding

(1 yard) Decorative trim ribbon

Craft glue

Drill/drill bits

Ink pads

Matte medium

Rubber stamp image

Tapestry needle

Vintage ledger pages

White kraft box, 10"x 8"x 8"

The snow falls in winter.
The flowers grow in <u>summer</u>.
(summers)

summer
sum-mer
summer
summer

The <u>sun</u> is in the sky.
We see the <u>sun</u> in the daytime.
The <u>sun</u> makes us warm.

sun
sun
sun

Letters from Home

These boxes contain letters received and paper with envelopes for letters yet to be sent.

(1 yard) Wire-edged ribbon

Acrylic paints

Alphabet rubber stamps

Cigar box, 7"x 5"x 2"

Clean dry cloth

Craft glue

Decorative self-adhesive label

Glue stick

Ink pads

Ledger pages

Matte medium

Postage stamp

Spray mount

Vintage postcard

1. Paint outside of box to complement postcard image. *Note: I painted the sides of my box celery green and the lid inside and out with robin's egg blue.* Apply two to three coats, allowing to dry thoroughly between coats.

2. Cut ledger page to frame postcard. Set aside. Cut additional ledger pages into 1" triangle border. Apply to top outside perimeter with matte medium, allowing to wrap around corners as necessary. Press firmly with cloth.

3. Dab two spots of craft glue at top and bottom centers of box. Wrap wire-edged ribbon around box, pressing down on these glue spots to hold firmly in place. Leave 12" ribbon loose on each end.

4. Apply ledger paper to box lid with matte medium, positioning over ribbon. Affix postcard into center with spray mount. Press firmly.

5. Adhere postage stamp to top corner of postcard with a glue stick.

6. Stamp label with the words "letter box." Affix onto inside of lid.

7. Apply ledger page border to top inside of lid with matte medium.

8. Tie box with a voluptuous bow with loose ribbon ends.

A Collection of Treasures

Black construction paper
Children's book
Matte medium
Pinking shears
Tea tins

Give a tin to each of your children to collect rocks, shells, and ticket stubs on your summer vacations.

1. Color-copy pages from a favorite children's book. Measure height of each tea tin and cut pages horizontally to fit. Include fun illustrations or chapter titles.

2. Apply to tin with matte medium. Begin at back and allow focal-point piece to overlap as needed.

3. Using pinking shears, cut construction paper slightly larger than lid. Apply with matte medium.

4. Color-copy alphabet from children's book, enlarging or reducing as necessary to fit. Apply a letter to center of construction paper with matte medium.

Music Box

Use this special box to collect keepsakes.

Black photo corners

Black tassel

Cardstock

Double-stick tape

Glitter

Matte medium

Newsprint

Scallop-edged scissors

Sheet music book with black border

Unused medium pizza box

1. Tear full sheets from a music book and apply to pizza box with matte medium. Apply at interesting angles, allowing pages to overlap as needed. Wrap entire surface of box inside and out; pressing air bubbles out with cloth.

2. Cut interesting title from music sheets. Apply music book cover to top of box. Overlap with title in center and capture all corners with photo corners.

3. Cut cardstock to fit front flap of box, allowing scallops to extend over the edge. Punch a hole at bottom of center scallop.

4. Set on top of newsprint and cover thoroughly with matte medium. Sprinkle a generous amount of glitter onto cardstock, gently tapping any excess off onto newsprint.

5. Pull tassel loop through hole and tie at the back.

6. Affix glittered scallop to front flap with double-stick tape, gently pressing into place.

There's No Place Like Home

(6") Rayon ribbon

(8") Wire-edged ribbon

Black matte spray paint

Buttons

Cardstock/heavy paper

Craft glue

Decorative-edged scissors

Matte medium

Metal lunch box

Old key

Old photograph

Pinking shears

Quote ribbon "there's no place like home"

Title page from book

Fill with brownies for your children when they get home from school.

1. Spray-paint metal lunchbox. Sand at edges to show age.

2. Apply title page to outside center of lunchbox lid with matte medium. Press on firmly with cloth.

3. Color-copy photograph onto cardstock or heavy paper. Trim with decorative-edged scissors. Apply to center of title page with matte medium.

4. Using pinking shears, trim "There's no place like home" from ribbon to fit at bottom edge of photo and adhere with craft glue. Decorate top border of photo with buttons. *Note: I began in the center and worked out to the edges to ensure even spacing between buttons.*

5. Loop rayon ribbon through key and tie to handle of lunchbox. Tie a one-sided bow with wire-edged ribbon around this loop.

Another Idea

{ If using a rectangular lunchbox, paste title page and photo to inside of lid so it can be seen when the box is open. }

The Places I've Been

Alphabet rubber stamps

Architectural renderings

Ink pads

Kraft "pencil" box, 12"x 4"x 3"

Matte medium

Mother-of-pearl belt buckle

Straight pin

Tea-dyed cotton twill, 36"x 1"

Fill this box with pens, colored pencils, tape, and a glue stick to record memories while traveling.

1. Cut out interesting elements from architectural renderings.

2. Create a collage on box lid, using matte medium. Layer your pieces at various angles, allowing them to wrap around to inside of box lid. To attain neat corners, fold paper at edges as if wrapping a gift. Press out all air bubbles with a soft cloth.

3. Wrap cotton twill lengthwise around box and capture the belt buckle. Secure into place with straight pin.

4. Rubber-stamp words onto cotton twill. *Note: Think of words that reflect the use of your box: traveling, writing, drawing, etc.*

IX

RÉ-QUI-SI-TION!

Chapter Three

Inside the Box

L'Atelier

Inside the Box

These projects are about telling a particular story within the framework of the box. In some cases the boxes' integrity has been maintained, such as the shadowboxes, which utilize the traditional format of creating a composition behind glass. Other projects literally set the notion of the box on its side. Playing with different positions may reveal nooks or compartments that can be explored as shelves or stacked with pieces from one's collection.

No. 194
6 Designs.

Harbinger of Spring

My friends and I do a craft project each May Day. This box celebrates our circle of friendship and the coming of spring.

1. Apply one coat black acrylic paint to crate.

2. Enlarge or reduce painting reproduction to fit inside of box. *Note: My theme is spring so I chose "Three Graces" by Boticelli. Apply to inside back of box with matte medium. Allow image to wrap around sides if desired.*

3. Stand box up vertically and wrap tulle around box horizontally. Begin at the bottom and wrap around toward the top, overlapping slightly at various angles.

4. Using safety pin, secure end of tulle to itself at back of box.

5. Gently separate the tulle at one of the overlap points and drop rose petals in so they fall to the bottom of the box.

6. Lay box on its back. Trim gimp to three pieces: one to fit the width at bottom of box and one for each side.

7. Hot-glue gimp to sides and bottom. Press firmly into place on front edge of box. *Note: This will simultaneously secure the tulle.*

8. Cut embroidered trim slightly wider than box. Secure at each corner with brass pins.

9. Glue rosebuds gently into place at top of box.

(1 yard) Bronze gimp

Black acrylic paint

Black-and-white painting reproduction

Brass escutcheon pins

Dried rosebuds and rose petals

Embroidered trim

Hot-glue gun

Light chartreuse tulle, 6"x 42"

Matte medium

Safety pin

Wooden crate, 7"x 11½"x 2"

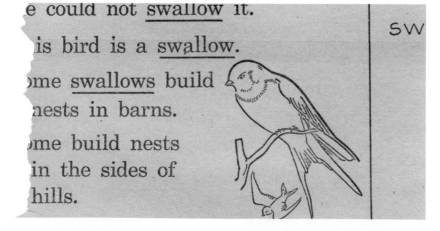

That Day the Circus Came to Town

Animal photo

Cigar box

Corrugated cardboard

Craft glue

Craft stick

Double-stick tape

Hot-glue gun

Ledger paper

Matte medium

Old circus peanut cans

Playing cards

Pom-pom trim

Sepia photograph

Striped paper bag

White acrylic paint

Various embellishments: buttons, dominoes, leaves, paper

I found these striped peanut cans at a flea market and decided to build a story around the memory they evoked.

1. Whitewash inside of cigar box and allow to dry.

2. Apply ledger paper with matte medium to cover inside of box and lid. Look for interesting patterns made with lines or words.

3. Affix animal photo with double-stick tape. Allow base of picture to curl up against box floor to create dimension.

4. Integrate where photo edges and box meet by gluing a domino and button at corners.

5. Tuck craft stick identifying the name of your animal into striped paper bag and affix to back of box with double-stick tape.

6. Cut pom-pom trim to width of box lid. Adhere to lid's top edges with craft glue.

7. Color-copy photograph. Cut a piece of corrugated cardboard slightly smaller than photo and adhere them together with glue stick. *Note: This will add dimension.*

8. Capture within photo corners and adhere to inside of lid with craft glue.

9. Add paper words or designs to reflect the story that is being told. Apply to box lid with matte medium.

10. Hot-glue box atop one peanut can. Glue another can to top of box. *Note: Box will stay balanced if can on top is placed slightly to the left.*

11. Insert a large thread spool into bottom of can. Hot-glue playing cards in place. *Note: This will allow the cards to rest at jaunty angles.*

12. Rest leaf loosely on top can for color.

An Afternoon in the Park

I collected both natural and found objects while strolling through Golden Gate Park one afternoon. Creating a collage with them was a perfect way to preserve the day.

Architectural rendering

Assorted paper ephemera

Bird image

Black string

Blue paper

Brass escutcheon pins

Craft glue

Dried leaves

Fabric trim

Ink pads

Matte medium

Metal edging

Playing card

Paper scraps

Robin's egg blue acrylic paint

Rubber stamp images

Shadowbox, 9"x 12"x 3"

Wooden plant labels, 4"

1.   Remove glass from shadowbox.

2.   Paint outside of shadowbox.

3.   Adhere blue paper to inside back of box with matte medium. *Note: Mine is a collage page found at the craft store.*

4.   Artfully tear edges of architectural rendering and apply over blue paper with matte medium.

5.   Creatively arrange ephemera in box. *Note: I included pieces that reminded me of a certain afternoon: an entry ticket to the conservatory, floral stamps, bird images, and a playing card found on the sidewalk. Reduce or enlarge ephemera on a color copier to adjust their size. Apply all pieces in place with matte medium.*

6.   Stamp wooden plant labels with identifying words. Adhere with craft glue, pressing firmly.

7.   Attach brass pins at various locations inside the box. Tie black string around one and follow to each pin to create an interesting pattern. Loop string once around each pin and tie off at last location.

8.   Carefully spread dried leaves at bottom of box, providing full coverage.

9.   Insert glass back into shadowbox.

10.   Secure metal edging to back sides of box with brass pins. Pinch together at front edge of box.

11.   Cut fabric to wrap across front and sides of box.

Tip

{ Making color copies of your images is not only useful for size adjustments but also preserves the originals. }

FLEURS   GOLDEN GATE

RIES   TICKET   984753
JUL 15 A.M.   MMF INDUSTRIES

COOL GRAPERY

OISEAUX

2 ♣

43

The Games We Used to Play

(3) Nails, ⅝"

(4) Wooden spools

Acrylic paints: ochre, parchment

Black shoe polish

Cardboard game box

Cotton string

Double-stick tape

Hot-glue gun

Old photograph

Rubber ball

Sandpaper

Vintage game cards: bingo, Monopoly, word games

Vintage game pieces: bingo chips, dominoes, jacks

Wooden cigar box, 6"x 7"x 2"

A small bag filled with old game pieces that I found at a garage sale became the starting point for this box. It reminds me of afternoons spent on the front porch of my grandfather's house playing with the neighborhood children.

1. Paint entire box inside and out with a wash of ochre acrylic. When dry, apply an uneven wash of parchment. Rub sections on or off with your fingers. Using a dry brush, apply ochre to certain areas and blend all. Sand lightly at edges.

2. Insert cardboard game box within borders of lid. *Note: It can fit snugly or be attached with double-stick tape.*

3. Secure photograph to left side of cardboard game box with three nails. Photo can then curl forward for dimension.

4. Using small dabs of hot glue, perch two jacks at base of inserted game box. Do the same with the word games card, angling slightly.

5. Affix Monopoly card to bingo card with double-stick tape, then sew together using a needle and thread.

6. Affix top edge of bingo card inside base of box with double-stick tape.

7. Wind the wooden spool with cotton string; be sure to leave 12" of string loose for rethreading within the vignette you have created. Hot-glue domino, word cube, and wooden spool to bottom edge of box base. *Note: You may also choose to simply place the game pieces on the box ledge as opposed to gluing them down. This allows for interaction with the box or rearranging at will.* Perch small rubber ball at top of string spool.

8. Using black shoe polish, rub two of the remaining spools to a light stain.

9. Hot-glue all remaining spools to bottom edges of box.

A Bird's Nest

Shadowboxes are a perfect format within which to explore a certain theme or passion. Each can hold a small vignette or crystallize a moment in time.

Assorted paper ephemera:
bird images, colored pages,
maps, playing cards, Buttons

Craft glue

Double-stick tape

Matte medium

Mint acrylic paint

Pom-pom trim

Scrabble letters

Several yards 28-gauge copper
wire

Shadowbox, 7½"x 5½"x 3"

Twigs

1. Remove back of shadowbox.

2. Paint outside of box to complement imagery that will be on the inside. *Note: I used a mint acrylic to match my chosen ephemera.*

3. Trim map paper to fit interior sides of shadowbox, applying one side at a time with matte medium. Press into place with cloth.

4. Compose collage on back inside panel of box, beginning with map paper. Arrange your elements before gluing into place. *Note: The panel lifts out to make it easier for you.* Apply collage elements to backboard, with matte medium, tearing some edges for interesting effect. *Note: For this box, the bird card is attached with a paper clip and held into place with double-stick tape.*

5. Adhere button with craft glue, then wind thread around button.

6. Roll several yards of copper wire in your hands to form a ball. Indent center to create small nest shape. Adhere in place with craft glue.

7. Place twigs gently inside and replace back of shadowbox.

8. Trim pom-poms to width of box and adhere to upper border with craft glue. Adhere button and Scrabble letters in the same manner.

Family of Six

The photograph of this woman spoke to me of someone who raised her family with dignity and pride. I kept the box simple to maintain this feeling.

(2) Leaf charms

Button

Copper nail

Corrugated cardboard

Craft glue

Glue stick

Ledger page

Matte medium

Old wooden frame,
6" square, 1"–2" deep

Sepia photograph

Storybook with names

Suspender clip

Thumbtack

1. Remove back and glass from frame. *Note: Back of frame should have nice torn details from original backing; leave those.*

2. Trim corrugated cardboard so that it fits snugly into frame opening. *Note: This will be your new background piece for your collage.*

3. Trim ledger page to fit cardboard and apply with matte medium.

4. Photocopy words from storybook to reflect thoughts of family—mention names if desired. Adhere to ledger page with a glue stick, pressing gently into place.

5. Capture photograph with suspender clip.

6. Secure to cardboard back with thumbtack. Adhere vintage button to top of tack with craft glue.

7. Replace glass into frame by setting lower half of glass at bottom outer edge of frame. Allow top of glass to simply fall back against background. *Note: This way, the glass perches within the frame at an angle.*

8. Secure two leaf charms to top border of frame with a copper tack.

Tip

{ In order to make sure the corrugated cardboard fit into my frame opening, I set the glass on top of the cardboard and traced around it with a pencil. }

ell. An ornamental mantel.

til-uh) *n.* A veil or headscarf
houlders,
h women.
s) *n.* [*pl.*
voracious
holds its
as if pray-

t'l) *n.*
se outer
it sleeves.
hat which
conceals.
hich gives
ing when
flame.—*v.*
an·tling]
guise; obscure. **2.** To become
ed, as with scum. **3.** To blush.
hoo-uh) *n.* A loose robe or
worn by women.

MANTILLA

The farmer had some new plants.

They were fine new plants.

One day Derk threw a ball.

The ball went over the gate.

Calling Card Box

Oftentimes, the simplest ideas are the best!

Craft glue

Calling cards

Floral frogs

Old tin box

Ribbon trim

Shoe polish (optional)

Vintage button

1. If you are lucky, your "old tin box" will have a wonderful artful patina of age to it. If not, you can rub with shoe polish to stain, hammer a bit for dents and sand at the edges.

2. Choose a card for the "title" of box. *Note: I liked the oval shape of this one.* Using craft glue, adhere to inside center of box lid. If lid isn't perfectly flat, simply glue down one portion of card.

3. Adhere button to card with craft glue.

4. Trim ribbon to length of lid, then adhere with a thin line of craft glue.

5. Place floral frogs inside box to capture remaining calling cards.

Expecting

Acrylic paint (optional)

Assorted collage papers

Button card

Cardboard

Ceramic letter

Cloth tape-measure snippet

Craft glue

Double-stick tape

Fabric trim snippets

Flash card

Hot wax

Hot-glue gun

Ink pads

Manila tags

Matte medium

Milliner's straight pin

Old pages (optional)

Old tin box, 5"x 12"x 4½"

Ribbon

Rubber stamp images

Sand

Test tube bottle with cork

Torn paper bag

Watch face

Wooden clothespin

This box grew from the rubber-stamped "angel babies" images. They reminded me of children born and angels unborn, and how we live in the balance of both.

1. Leave tin as found if it has appealing idiosyncrasies. Otherwise, you may give it a random wash of acrylic paint or glue old pages to some of the sides and rip away pieces when partially dry.

2. Stamp manila tags with "angel baby" image. *Note: My theme is loosely based upon the anticipation of birth.* Attach one tag to box lid with clothespin, and insert second into paper bag.

3. Cut cardboard to fit snugly within box interior. Affix the paper bag to cardboard with double-stick tape.

4. Adhere fabric trim snippets to top and bottom borders of paper bag with craft glue. *Note: I added black eyelets and a milliner's pin to further the look of attachment.* Adhere button card to paper bag with craft glue.

5. Hot-glue wooden alphabet block to back of box. Hot-glue collage papers to the block. Press firmly. Allow "angel baby" tag string to dangle naturally over this suspended collage.

6. Adhere flash card to lid of box with craft glue; layer with the watch face and tape-measure snippet.

7. Partially fill test tube bottle with sand. Insert cork and wind ribbon around neck. Brush hot wax over cork to seal bottle.

8. Perch bottle and ceramic letter at base of box or hot-glue into place. *Note: All of these elements were chosen for their allusion to measuring time.*

The Books I've Read

I collect old books for the sheer beauty of their worn pages and watermarked covers. This box pays homage to all the books I have used and enjoyed throughout the years.

Black acrylic paint

Carpet tack

Copper hand

Craft glue

Fabric trim

Glass drawer pull

Hot-glue gun

Old books: 4"x 6" and 3"x 4"

Old wallpaper

Ruler

Shadowbox, 12"x 8"x 3"

String

Small eyelet

Wooden blocks

1. Paint inside and outside of box with two coats of black acrylic paint. When thoroughly dry, sand at edges for an aged quality.

2. Apply wallpaper piece to back of box with matte medium. Press firmly with cloth; fold back corner edges for additional interest.

3. Hot-glue two wooden spacer blocks to back center of box.

4. Partially disassemble larger book by loosening some pages and allowing to stick out at top.

5. Adhere fabric trim at top of book with small dabs of craft glue.

6. Hot-glue book to spacer blocks, with sufficient glue to hold firmly in place.

7. Open smaller book to a favorite page and adhere to larger book with craft glue. Lay flat and allow to dry overnight.

8. Attach glass drawer pull to center top of box, using its own hardware.

9. Secure copper hand to center of books using a carpet tack.

10. Screw eyelet into top of box and thread with 24" string. Wrap string around bottom edges of books and tie into place, tucking ends behind smaller book and wrapping once around carpet tack. *Note: This string functions to help hold the book in place.*

11. Cut a small wing-shaped fragment from book page and adhere into place between both books with craft glue.

12. Insert glass and adhere ruler to edge of box with craft glue.

Adelane's Tea

China cup

Copper nails

Craft glue

Deck of cards

Finial

Old photograph

Ribbons

Ruler

String

Used and unused tea bags

Wooden crate with three
dividers

*Did my grandmother even drink tea? I'm not
certain, but I like to imagine she did.*

1. Stand box up on one end. Secure finial to top
   side of the box with a nail or screw.

2. Secure photograph to focal side of box with two
   copper nails.

3. Adhere ruler to bottom corner of box with
   craft glue.

4. Stack used tea bags neatly at left side of top
   "shelf." Let strings dangle naturally. Fill in right
   side of shelf by stacking new tea bags.

5. Tie ribbons around finial and let ends fall over
   tea bags.

6. Wrap one tea-bag string between copper nails
   at photograph.

7. Tie playing cards together with string and lay on
   middle shelf.

8. Place china teacup on lower shelf, allowing tea-
   bag strings to dangle inside.

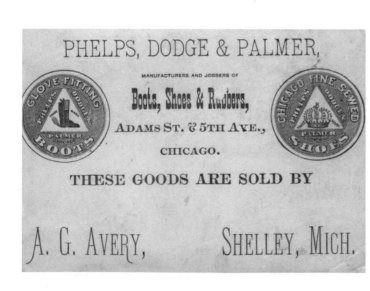

Anastazia & Josef

This box commemorates my grandmother and grandfather, who immigrated to this country in the early 1900s. I keep small books and letters inside, which are reminiscent of them.

22-gauge wire

Clothespin

Craft glue

Favorite quote trim

Grosgrain trim

Matte medium

Old maps

Postcard

Sepia photograph

Spray mount

Stencil

Suspender clips

Tin box, 8"x 5"x 4"

Vintage buttons

Vintage silk hankie

1. Using matte medium, cover outside of box and inside of lid with maps. Tear to fit before gluing.

2. Wrap wire around corner of box lid and attach to front corner of box with a clothespin to keep box in the open position.

3. Find or rubber-stamp names of ancestors being commemorated.

4. With spray mount, affix photograph (or use a copy on photo paper) to center of lid interior.

5. Layer quote over photograph with matte medium.

6. Adhere a button at quote corner and another at front center of box with craft glue. Spot-glue the top of the stencil to the box while letting the base rest on the lip of the box lid. *Note: This will create more depth.*

7. Attach postcard to back center of box with suspender clips.

8. Spread craft glue at top border of box lid. Trim grosgrain ribbon to fit and press firmly into place.

9. Tie silk hankie to tin box clasp and allow to drape naturally.

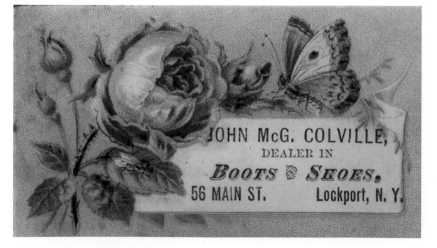

A Day at the Beach

Bingo pieces

Blue acrylic paint

Craft glue

Double-stick tape

Flash card

Hot-glue gun

Large sheet wrapping paper

Matte medium

Paper umbrella

Postage stamps

Rickrack

Seashells

Shadowbox, 7½"x 6"x 3"

Vintage beach postcards

I look inside this shadowbox and dream on otherwise dreary days.

1. Paint entire outside of box.

2. Cover inside sides of box by trimming wrapping paper to fit and applying with matte medium. Press firmly with cloth.

3. Arrange collage on board back of shadowbox. Cover entire surface with wrapping paper. Affix flash card with double-stick tape. Adhere stamps to flash card with craft glue.

4. Hot-glue one bingo piece into place as a collage element and two as spacer pieces to elevate the postcard.

5. Hot-glue postcard to spacers, pressing firmly into place. Affix additional collage elements, a dated paper scrap, and front corner from another postcard with double-stick tape.

6. Fill bottom shelf of shadowbox with seashells. Prop umbrella slightly open by securing with a small piece of tape at handle. Insert at angle amongst shells.

7. Adhere remaining seashells to top of box with a generous amount of craft glue.

8. Trim rickrack to fit front edges of shadowbox. Adhere with small dabs of craft glue, pressing firmly into place.

Tip

{ Attach wooden drawer pulls to top of box in place of seashells for a vintage look. }

Chapter Four

All Around the Box

All Around the Box

This chapter is about exploring the box as an entirely new format. Often, unusual choices are made, such as the old birdcage or the glass cloche. Other times, the box simply becomes a blank canvas, a flat multifaceted surface upon which to explore a particular idea. It can be painted, waxed, or collaged to completely alter its texture or to preserve areas that are already visually appealing. This allows an interesting interplay to occur. Hung inside out on a wall, a box may become a hinged diptych ready to accept one's story.

Boulevard

Items collected on a trip to Paris come together on the back of this wooden box to create a small wall piece.

Assorted ephemera:
botanicals, postcards, stamps

Beeswax

Button

Construction grade wood,
36" x 1" x 2"

Hammer

Ink pad

Ledger paper

Matte medium

Nails

Plywood piece, 7" x 8"

Rubber stamp images

Saw

String

Thumbtacks

Wooden chip brush

1. Build stretcher bar:

    a.) Cut two 8" x 1" x 2" pieces and two 5" x 1" x 2" pieces from wood.

    b.) Nail together at sides to create a small square.

    c.) Lay plywood piece flat atop stretcher bar and nail into place.

2. Using matte medium, cover entire front and sides with ledger paper.

3. Play with the elements of your collage before gluing into place. *Note: Think about including a larger focal point and working within a limited color palette.*

4. When pleased with the composition, apply pieces into place with matte medium, overlapping papers at various angles.

5. Thicker pieces of ephemera (in this case a postcard) can be secured with nails or thumbtacks. Tie black string between the two to integrate.

6. Cover entire piece with a beeswax layer.

Baby's New Nest

It felt strange at first to place this photograph within a cage, so I transformed it into a cozy nest where anyone might feel welcome.

(3) Small silver eyelets

22-gauge copper wire

Baby alphabet bead bracelet

Baby photo (new or vintage)

Birdcage (new or used)

Children's wooden alphabet blocks

Clothespins

Dried/velvet flower

Matte medium

Mini clothespins

Sandpaper

Stencil initial

Textbook

White raffia ribbon

Wire-edged ribbon

1. Paint birdcage to reflect gender of baby and allow to dry. Sand lightly at edges for an aged look.

2. Using matte medium, cover wooden blocks with text, folding edges over as if wrapping a gift. For a smooth finish, coat blocks with matte medium.

3. Insert eyelet into center of block and tie with ribbon bow.

4. String baby's name and the word "celebrate" or "Bambino," onto copper wires. Set "celebrate" wire aside. Secure name to photo with mini clothespins. If using a new photo, apply first to a piece of cardstock with matte medium. *Note: Photo must be sturdy enough to stand on its own.*

5. Fill back of birdcage with raffia.

6. Hang one wooden block "gift" to top of cage. Tie bow at top and insert flower.

7. Prop door open by inserting wire-edged ribbon though vertical bars and tying a generous bow.

8. Attach "celebrate" wire in an artful manner to outside of birdcage. Allow wire ends to twist and turn and corkscrew at far edges.

9. Capture stencil initial in clasp that used to hold the door shut, or simply hot-glue stencil in place.

10. Place wooden block "gifts" on floor of baby's new nest.

To Italy & Back

I collected so many wonderful pieces of ephemera on our trip to Italy, collaging cigar boxes was my way of making certain my collection would be exposed and enjoyed.

(2) Cigar boxes

Acrylic paints: ochre, terra-cotta

Copper nails

Copper wire

Craft glue

Gold leaf

Matte medium

Spray mount

Various Italian ephemera: maps, painting reproductions, postcards, stamps

Velvet ribbon

1. Paint ochre and terra-cotta washes over both boxes. Allow interesting sections of box to show through.

2. Tear ephemera to manageable shapes and sizes. Apply to various sections of the boxes with matte medium. *Note: Keep in mind that larger images can cover up any areas you're not sure of. Try to vary scale and consider maintaining a certain color palette as you choose your elements.*

3. Spray-mount two art reproductions onto top box; use an ornate music border to give it a new frame. The bottom art piece becomes framed by hammering copper nails into three corners, threading thin copper wire along the top border, and adhering velvet ribbon to the bottom border with craft glue.

4. Gold-leaf areas of box, following manufacturer's instructions. *Note: I used gold leaf to lightly adhere the box shut as well as to highlight borders and areas where various ephemera cross each other.*

5. Create a true three-dimensional piece by placing one box on top of another.

Girl's Night Out

(3) Typeset blocks

Black acrylic paint

Craft glue

Decorative paper/vintage wallpaper

Definition photocopied from dictionary

Dominoes

Floral frog

Folding measuring stick

Glue stick

Hot-glue gun

Lace scraps

Matte medium

Small book, 6"x 4"

Small manila tag

Thumbtacks

Velvet ribbon

Vintage flower or leaf

Vintage photo

Wooden clothespin

Wooden crate, 10"x 8"x 2½"

Wooden doorknob

The photo of these women reminded me of my own special friendships, and I wanted them to feel they could cavort once again, if only within this little art piece.

1. Paint outside of crate black.

2. Paint checkerboard pattern on front sides; sand edges when dry.

3. Trim wallpaper to fit inside back of crate; apply with matte medium and press firmly into place.

4. Open up book to an interesting page; secure cover of book to back of crate with thumbtack. Allow book to stand loosely ajar inside the box.

5. Using a clothespin, secure photograph to pages of book. Label photo with photocopied definition. Adhere to photo with glue stick.

6. Trim velvet ribbon to fit bottom border of box. Adhere with small dots of craft glue.

7. Hot-glue dominoes to top of box. Place the center one first, then work out toward sides.

8. Using small dabs of craft glue, gently press trimmed lace scrap just underneath dominoes to edge of crate.

9. Hot-glue three wooden typeset blocks to function as legs for crate.

10. Unfold measuring stick and allow to fall through the slots in the crate. Outer edges of stick will rest on the crate.

11. Perch floral frog at left side of book; insert small manila tag that has been embellished with vintage flower or leaf.

12. Allow stem to wind gracefully within the box. Secure flower into the pages with clothespin.

13. Hot-glue wooden doorknob to domino.

Crowned

This small art piece can be displayed in a vintage tin "pedestal," which helps draw attention to the art piece itself.

Beeswax
Black acrylic
Book page
Ink pads
Khaki acrylic
Matte medium
Rubber stamp images
Vintage tin
Water bottle cap
White paper
Wooden block, 3"x 5"x 1"

1. Apply white paper to face of block, with matte medium. Apply text border from book to top of one block and press flat with cloth. *Note: My border is from a Spanish ledger book.*
2. Rubber-stamp images onto front of block.
3. Paint sides and back of block with khaki acrylic.
4. Cover face and sides of block with beeswax. To make circles, dip rim of a water bottle cap into black acrylic and press firmly into the wax to leave impressions. Fill one circle in with more black paint and coat it with khaki, then partially rub off to create a layered effect.
5. Place art piece on vintage tin.

80
George Brown
5/ 31 Paid .25
6/ 11 Paid 7/6 .85
7/ 11 1.75
7/ 19 3.90
credit by eggs .82
7/ 20 .10
7/ 22 .45
7/ 25 1.58
paid 8/ 31
9/ 16 3.82

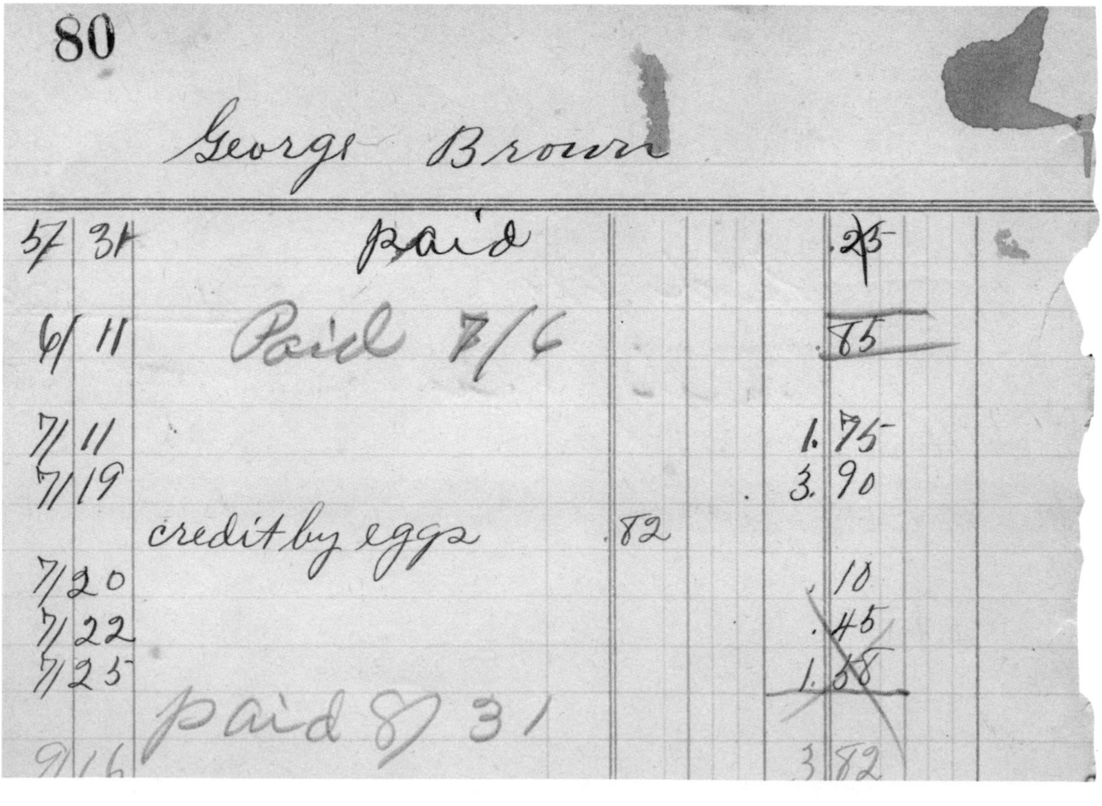

73

Rainy Day

The juxtaposition of the school text and stamped raincoat image reminded me of long-ago days spent stomping in puddles and twirling my umbrella on my way to grade school.

(2) Thread spools

Acrylic paints: pink, black

Beeswax

Construction-grade wood, 36"x 1"x 2"

Copper nail

Craft glue

Grade school textbook

Ink pads

Matte medium

Nails

Plywood, 7"x 8"

Rubber stamp images

Wooden beads

Wooden block, 5"x 5"x 1"

Frame

1. Make stretcher bar frame. Cut two 8"x1"x2" pieces and two 5"x1"x2" pieces from wood.

2. Nail together to create a small square. Lay plywood piece flat atop stretcher bar and nail into place on back side.

3. Paint sides and back of frame black. Create a checkerboard pattern around border with loose painterly strokes. When thoroughly dry, sand entire frame. Wipe clean.

4. Apply schoolbook text to back and lower edge of frame with matte medium, pressing firmly with cloth.

Insert

1. Apply a page of text to wooden block with matte medium.

2. Rubber-stamp images onto block firmly and boldly.

3. Paint sides and back of block with pink acrylic. Let dry.

4. Coat entire front and sides of block with beeswax.

5. Secure picture hanger to back of block and hang on copper nail within frame.

6. Adhere wooden beads to top of frame and to thread spools at bottom with craft glue. Press all firmly into place and allow to dry overnight.

See the rain.
Jane likes the rain.
She takes a raincoat.
She goes to the gate.

43

Botanical Blocks

Use these solid blocks as fabulous bookends.

Beeswax

Cut-out tag

Italian and French textbooks
with illustrations, 4"x 3" and
4½"x 4"

Matte medium

Paper ephemera

Postage stamps

Rayon ribbon

String

1. Rip pages from books, including interesting illustrations. Tear these into smaller, more manageable pieces.

2. Using matte medium, cover entire block with text as if wrapping a present.

3. Build your collage over this background, layering words and illustrations. Allow edges to wrap around sides and create focal points on top and sides of block.

4. Apply beeswax to all sides of the block except bottom. Begin at the top and allow wax to run down sides. Excess drips can be scraped away with a razor blade edge.

5. Cut rayon ribbon to twice the circumference of the block and tie a loose bow.

6. Cover cut-out tag with various paper ephemera and attach with string.

abcdefghijklmnopqrstuvwxyz. 1234567890.

Chaucer. Caxton. Spencer. Shakspeare.

Vere Foster's Copy Books — Nº 10.　　　　BLACKIE AND SON, PRINTERS, DUBLIN.

Stage Set Cloche

(8") Glass cloche

(15") French wire-edged ribbon

Acrylic varnish

Black acrylic paint

Craft glue

Fabric trim

Matte medium

Music sheet

Velvet leaves

Wooden disk, 10"x ½"

Use this ensemble to showcase a special collection.

1. Paint bottom and sides of disk black.

2. Trace disk onto sheet music and trim to fit. Apply to disk top with matte medium, smoothing out with a cloth.

3. Brush with two coats of varnish, allowing to dry between coats.

4. Adhere fabric trim around circumference of disk with craft glue.

5. Loop French ribbon once around handle of cloche. Place velvet leaf stem in center of loop and capture while tying the bow. Add additional snippets of ribbon for extra flair.

Tip

{ Substitute a silver tray for the wooden disk, for a more elegant look. }

My Own Backyard

Setting this storage box upright to create shelves, I layered it with objects like those which surround me in my studio and garden. In this way I am always reminded of "home."

Acrylic paints: ochre, white

Bird's nest

Buttons

Craft glue

Decorative-edged scissors

Glue stick

Hot-glue gun

Ink pads

Ivory paper

Plastic egg

Rubber stamp images

Small old bottle

Tape measure

Thumbtack

Used tin

Velvet leaves

Wooden alphabet block

Wooden crate with two dividers, 8"x 14"x 3½"

1. Paint entire box with two coats of white acrylic. When mostly dry, sand edges. Stand crate on end.

2. Adhere tape measure to top border of box with craft glue.

3. Paint a thin coat of ochre acrylic on egg and partially rub off with fingers before completely dry.

4. Hot-glue egg and wooden alphabet block into place.

5. Gently lay nest on middle shelf.

6. Label bottle and tin by stamping associative words on ivory paper. Trim with decorative-edged scissors, then adhere to surfaces with glue stick. Scratch away areas of the labels for a used look.

7. Place bottle and tin on bottom shelf. *Note: Tin can be used to collect small treasures from your own backyard: feathers, pinecones, stones.*

8. Secure velvet leaf grouping to top corner with a thumbtack. Corkscrew stems around your finger. Adhere small button to head of tack with craft glue.

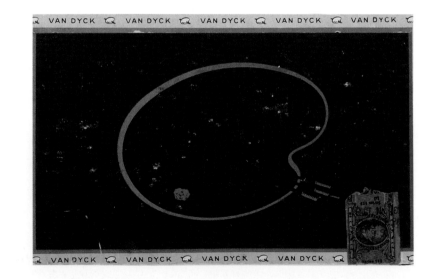

Love Letter Frame

The handwriting and postage on old letters can be so lovely, they deserve a display of their own.

Cigar box

Craft glue

Crafter's knife

Decorative paper

Eyelet

Hand-tinted photo

Hot-glue gun

Love letters and various paper ephemera

Matte medium

Pinking shears

Rickrack

Safety pin

Sea-grass green acrylic paint

Silk ribbon

Straight pins

String

Stuffed heart keepsake

Velvet leaves/flowers

1. Carefully remove lid of cigar box with a crafter's knife and discard.

2. Paint entire box inside and out with acrylic. Allow to dry.

3. Create collage inside box by layering torn pieces from a love letter and other decorative paper memorabilia. *Note: Keep in mind a general color scheme and include a hand-tinted photo that has been torn to create a new shape.* Apply all into place with matte medium, pressing firmly cloth.

4. Attach eyelet slightly off-center to top of box. Attach stuffed heart or other keepsake by looping silk ribbon through top of safety pin and eyelet, tying a secure bow. *Note: I used a vintage pincushion that had sentimental value and in which a safety pin easily fastened.*

5. Hammer straight pins into place, creating corner markers around photo.

6. Beginning at the upper-left pin, loop string once around each pinhead and tie a secure knot when arriving at the original pin. *Note: This will create a dimensional outline.*

7. Trim two 8½"x2" strips and two 5½"x2" strips from decorative paper. Draw a scallop pattern on the back of the paper and trim with pinking shears.

8. Working one side at a time, brush craft glue on cigar box edge and press paper to adhere.

9. Trim four pieces of rickrack to further adorn edges. Sparingly dab with craft glue and press gently into place. Make sure edge is kept straight.

10. Using craft glue, adhere velvet leaves and flowers at each corner where rickrack meets.

11. Cut two 15" lengths from silk ribbon. Turn box over onto its face and place a dot of hot glue near each upper corner. Press one end of ribbon on each spot. Turn box back over and tie a bow with remaining ends of ribbon.

My West Coast Aunts

Beeswax

Black string

Copper nails

Decorative-edged scissors

Family photographs

Large wooden beads

Ledger book

Matte medium

Plywood piece, 16"x 24"x ⅛"

Schoolbook text

White acrylic paint

My father had six siblings, four of which I referred to as my "West Coast Aunts." Each holds a special place in my heart; and I love how I can turn this box around and think of each individually.

1. Cut out six 8"-square boards, then nail together to create box.

2. Cover entire box with ledger paper, applying with matte medium and folding over sides as necessary.

3. Whitewash over paper, allowing some areas to show through.

4. Color-copy photos and trim with decorative-edged scissors. Apply to sides with matte medium.

5. Cut and apply words or names as appropriate. Play with scale and unusual placement to create interest.

6. Hot-glue large wooden beads, one to each corner of bottom of box.

7. Cover entire box with beeswax, beginning at the top and allowing wax to drip down sides. Do not wax the bottom.

8. Place nails at four locations around the photographs, being inventive in considering how you would like each picture framed.

9. Tie string around nails, making a loop around each one as you go and securing with a knot and bow at final nail.

Photo Day

I imagine the excitement and honor this young girl must have felt as she anticipated having her photograph taken. The box is layered with tokens from her special day.

28-gauge wire fragment

Acrylic paints: black, gold

Bingo piece

Brass escutcheon pins

Copper nail

Craft glue

Crown rubber stamp

Crystal drawer pull

Double-stick tape

Drill/drill bits

Eyelet

Ink pad

Ledger paper

Locker tag

Matte medium

Playing card

Ribbon snippets

Sepia photograph in cardstock frame

Sepia photograph, unframed

Skeleton key

Spray mount

Star charm

Tea-stained manila tag

Typewriter key

Upholstery tacks

Wooden box, 7"x 7"x 2"

Wooden domino

1. Paint box inside and out with black acrylic and allow to dry. Paint with a thin gold wash, rubbing some of the gold off with a dry cloth. Wash various areas with black and sand lightly when dry. *Note: This should give you a nicely aged surface.*

2. Open the box and lay it flat on table, inside face down. Turn the box so that the base is aligned over the lid.

3. Using matte medium, apply ledger page to center of box base (which is now at the top).

4. Affix framed photograph to ledger paper with spray mount. Secure top corners with upholstery tacks. *Note: This is for decorative as well as functional purposes.*

5. Affix unframed photograph, this time face down, to lid of box with spray mount. Hammer escutcheon pins to four corners.

6. Drill two small holes at base of first photograph, near the corners. Lay found wire piece across photo and tie into place by threading wire through the holes from the back.

7. Slide playing card behind photo frame and secure with a tack.

8. Use matte medium to apply small snippets of text to photo frame and at top edge of playing card.

9. Rubber-stamp a crown onto a manila tag. Tear bottom of tag off, then thread ribbon snippet through loop. Affix to photo with double-stick tape.

10. Secure star charm to the hand in the photograph with a copper nail.

11. Attach eyelet to bottom center of box. Attach key to the eyelet by threading with wire and tying into place. Add a ribbon bow and extra charm if desired.

12. Adhere locker tag and domino piece to the second photograph with craft glue. Layer and adhere the domino with an upside-down bingo piece and typewriter key. Allow to dry thoroughly.

13. Adhere glass drawer pull to top of box with craft glue.

Chapter
Five

Gallery
of Artists

53

Gallery of Artists

In the following chapter, nine artists have generously offered their own variations of memory boxes. Each explores the concept in a very unique and personal manner, creating pieces that are accessible yet extremely individual in nature. I love how a seemingly simple premise can lead to so many paths of exploration. I am honored to have such grand company.

Leaves No. 5762

Anne Cook

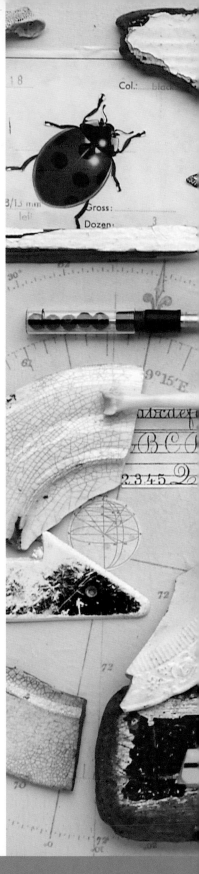

Anne Cook

is a successful collage artist and self-described "Bay Area Urban Archaeologist." She began collecting various items such as old lace, buttons, and heirlooms from flea markets, and estate and garage sales before discovering the beauty and use of beach debris. A vast array of both natural and manmade items—broken glass from a Coca-Cola bottle, shells, bleached animal bones, pottery shards, century-old knobs and machine dials from dated Bay Area factories—become details in the story her art unfolds. "What I see are shapes and patterns that have harmony and belong together visually, texturally, and by color. I assemble relics and remnants tossed out by the sea to create assemblages from found items that literally swirl around each of us." In addition to her collage work, Anne is an internationally recognized illustrator, designer, and jewelry maker. Accompanied by her dog, Anne beach-combs every chance she gets. Contact Anne at Anne@annecook.com.

Birch Portal

Apothecary

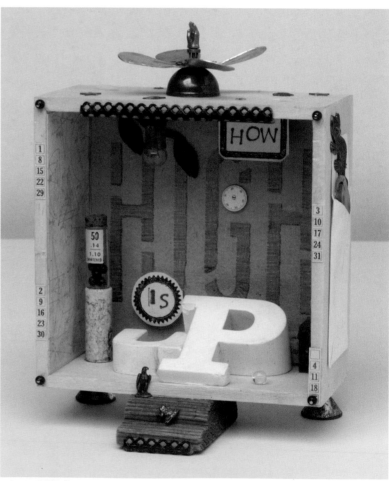

How High Is Up?

Anne Cook
continued

Illuminate

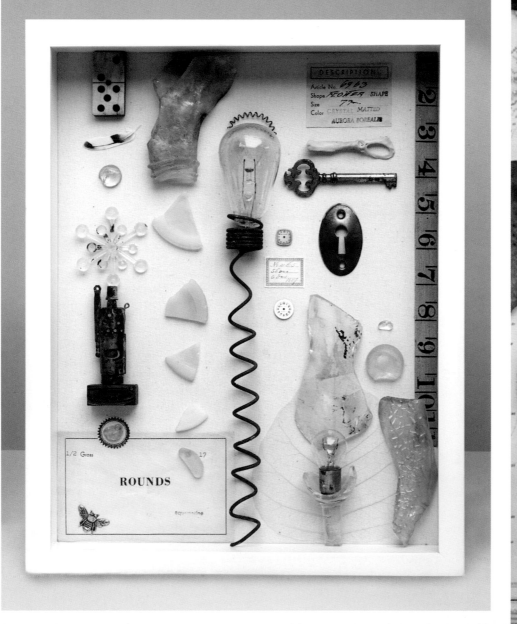

I Keep Your Letters

Gallery of Artists

Mindy Carpenter

Mindy Carpenter

is especially drawn to memory boxes due to her love of sending and receiving handmade envelopes, letters, and all forms of mail art. What better way to store precious correspondence than a handmade box? "I Keep Your Letters" is a frequent theme; it's at once intimate and inviting for the recipient. These are often some of her most cherished gifts for friends and family. For Mindy, the time spent on her art is an integral part of her world. "It's calming and rejuvenating. Boxes, collage, cards—all sorts of projects just pop into my head while I'm in my studio; but I have to be there for the magic to happen. Showing up counts for a lot." Her memory boxes, mail art, visual journals, and teaching schedule can be seen at www.mindycarpenter.com. Mindy Carpenter is the Creative Director for Cavallini Papers & Co. She lives with her husband Giovanni and her cat Sasha in Marin County, California.

Correspondence

Follow Your Bliss

Café Au Lait

Mindy Carpenter
continued

I Keep Your Letters II

Larkspur

Martha Johnson

Martha Johnson's
memory artwork incorporates her
sentimentality, nostalgia, and penchant
for collecting keepsakes and heirlooms.
Inspiration for these projects was found
throughout her home in such forms as
old photos, postcards, jewelry, crystal
perfume bottles, and antique china.
These pieces blend the nostalgic need to
create mood with her memorabilia.
Combining dated family photos with
color gives new life to old black-and-
whites, while forming a collage of a
family member's life artfully portrays
their story. Martha lives in Petaluma,
California, where she works as an artist
and art teacher. See more of her work at
http://home.att.net/~martharjohnson.

Aunt Momo's Gloves

Uncle Bob Built Chimneys

Martha Johnson
continued

Travel Life—Yakima to Medina

Fortunes for Success

Suzanne Young

Suzanne Young

is an artist from the Bay Area who has
held an interest in preserving memories
in special boxes since childhood. She
uses sentimental items in her pieces,
such as saved ticket stubs, a photograph,
a key, or a fortune from a cookie. These
objects are often accented by
representational devices: doorknobs as
access to the past or a locked box
symbolic of moments too personal to
share. Suzanne enjoys working in her
studio surrounded by bits and pieces of
her personal history. Her hope in
creating memory boxes is that, "the
collected items draw the viewer in and
stimulate their own memories and
feelings from the past." More of
Suzanne's work can be seen at
http://www.fauxpainting.us.

The Recycling Machine

Indulgence

Shrine to Obsession

Memory Box #3

Chela Fielding

Chela Fielding's

interest in memory boxes stems from her fascination with drawers as hiding places. She says, "We are constantly organizing, categorizing, folding, storing, labeling, and then usually shutting the lid or pushing in the drawer. I feel that when we look in, we are seeing a special place, something secret. Allowing light into these drawers and exposing certain objects is a wonderful opportunity to see." Chela is currently pursuing a Master of Fine Arts in the Sculpture Department at Massachusetts College of Art in Boston. She can be reached at chelalu@mindspring.com.

Memory Drawer #1

Memory Drawer #2

Memory Drawer #3

Chela Fielding
continued

Memory Drawer #4

Yakov

Grandmother Time

Valerie Raps

Valerie Raps

is a mixed-media artist who crafted the Light Box Series as an exploration into the miniature. Each box is composed of recycled materials that create tiny luminous environments. The variety of both personal items and found objects result in a rich visual texture; each component contributes its past and melds with the others to create new chapters. "The objects begin to take on a life of their own as they develop relationships to one another and their environment. Finally, each box is infused with light that brings the story to life." Valerie is currently working on her Master of Fine Arts degree in the Spatial Arts Department at San Jose State University in California. She can be reached at valraps@mindspring.com.

Boy and Dog

White Wall of Light

Birthday Box

Susan Gould

Susan Gould

has been fascinated by shadowboxes since the age of six. She enjoys the pursuit of worthy memory-box-making materials and feels fortunate to spend hours in junk stores as a part of her job description. Susan's company, Shadowbox, is a proud indicator of just how influential the concept is in her life. She says, "I create them, I collect them, I admire them, I love them." Susan is a self-taught artist with a background in graphic design. She currently resides in the San Francisco Bay Area. See more of her work at www.shaowboxart.com.

Wedding Box

Travel Box

Wooden Boxes

Susan Gould
continued

Happy Birthday to Kelly

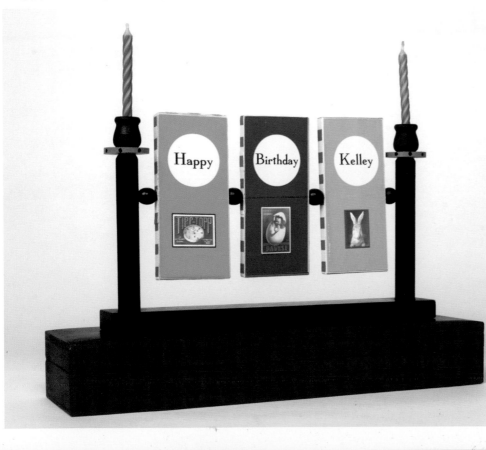

Rebecca Lundstrom Trawick

Southern California artist

Rebecca Lundstrom Trawick

has been the proprietor of Bluebird Studios since 1998, specializing in collage and hand-lettering. Her vintage-inspired collage work is comprised of found materials, paper ephemera, and other antiquated items reminiscent of a bygone era—one Rebecca didn't live through, but often dreams of. Her memory boxes take collage to a new level, drawing attention to detail both inside and out. Rebecca also works with brides across the US, and her hand-lettering style has left a funky, contemporary mark on hundreds of weddings. See additional work online at www.bluebirdstudios.com.

Jack's Memory Box, Age 6

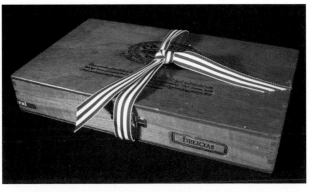

Susie's Memory Box, Age 5

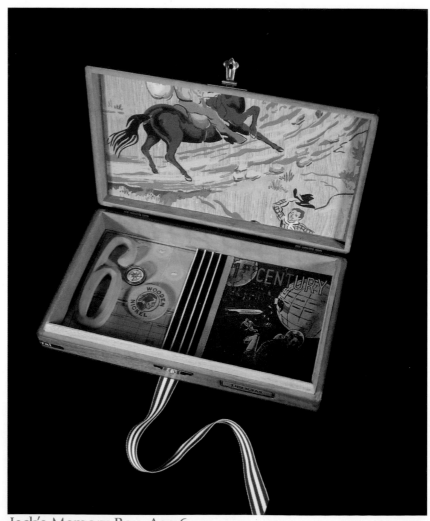

Jack's Memory Box, Age 6

Rebecca Lundstrom Trawick *continued*

Remembering Granny

The New Bride

Delisa Sage

Delisa Sage

is a mixed-media collage and mosaic artist. She uses handmade papers, vintage objects, broken dishes, and other found objects in her work. Delisa, a "flea-market junkie," scours the marketplace for all things dated: vintage game pieces, archaic photos and slides, worn boxes, and shrines. "I find the process of making memory boxes connects me with the past. Sometimes I imagine all the people who have used these things and what their stories might be." Delisa lives in Marin, California, and owns Collage Studio Gallery in San Francisco. See more work online at www.collagegallerysf.com.

Checkers, Anyone?

Butterfly Wings and Things

Delisa Sage
continued

Dancing on the Waves

About the Author

Anna Corba earned a degree in art history, but did not begin to paint until she returned to school to study fine arts. As an avid wanderer of flea markets, Anna's growing collection of paper ephemera, buttons, and oddball objects began to make its way into her paintings. Eventually, her work became more about collage than painting, so she developed a product line in which she could use these found objects. Anna's collaged journals, tags, bottles, and other home accessories are sold in specialty shops across the United States.

Anna is the author of *Vintage Paper Crafts, Memories of a Lifetime: Alphabets and Ornaments,* and *Instant Memories: Travel,* published by Sterling/Chapelle.

Anna works out of a carriage house studio next to her home in the rolling hills north of San Francisco. She lives with her husband, Nicolas, and her favorite four-legged creature, her dog Caylus.

Acknowledgments

This book has been an effort of many and I would like to thank each for their contribution.

Thank-you to Jo Packham and Cindy Stoeckl at Chapelle for continuing to create opportunities for artists to express themselves.

Thank-you, Steve Aja, for always being willing to go the extra mile to get the shot right.

Thank-you, Ana Maria Ventura, for your thoughtful attention to all details of this book. I always felt in good hands.

Thank-you, Molly Quoyser, for the magic of your shop, Mixing Whimsey, and opening your doors wide to receive our photo shoot. It couldn't have been a more delectable setting.

Thank-you, Kathy Lely, for your charming displays that made my photo-styling efforts that much easier.

Many, many thanks for the generosity of the women who comprise the Artists Gallery. I am honored to consider each a friend and kindred spirit.

Thank-you, Anne Cook, for finding the beauty in each of your found objects and caring enough to give them new homes. Also, for every peek inside your million-drawered studio—vastly inspiring!

Thank-you, Mindy Carpenter, for your sparkle and enthusiasm and luscious use of materials.

Thank-you, Martha Johnson, for always being willing to jump in the ring. How do I love thee more… fish tacos or painting? Hmm…

Thank-you, Suzanne Young, for your heartfelt ways with paper and paint. Long live trips to Europe!

Thank-you, Chela Fielding, for your intensity and dedication to your art.

Thank-you, Valerie Raps, for bothering to stumble upon my work in San Francisco and embracing it wholeheartedly. I enjoy watching your journey unfold.

Thank-you, Susan Gould, for making your presence known in your irrepressible way; from valentines to your whimsical product line, I'm with ya, baby!

Thank-you, Rebecca Trawick, for our postal trades and little mutual admiration society.

Thank-you, Delisa Sage, for revealing new layers every time I see your work, and for providing a fabulous venue for other artists at your ever-changing gallery.

Thank-you to my family for your continued support and belief in my abilities. Your pride and interest help me move forward.

And thank-you to my dear husband Nicolas, my true friend of friends, who understands the most what this journey means to me. You're still the one.

Metric Equivalency Charts

mm-millimeters cm-centimeters
inches to millimeters and centimeters

inches	mm	cm	inches	cm	inches	cm
1/8	3	0.3	9	22.9	30	76.2
1/4	6	0.6	10	25.4	31	78.7
1/2	13	1.3	12	30.5	33	83.8
5/8	16	1.6	13	33.0	34	86.4
3/4	19	1.9	14	35.6	35	88.9
7/8	22	2.2	15	38.1	36	91.4
1	25	2.5	16	40.6	37	94.0
1¼	32	3.2	17	43.2	38	96.5
1½	38	3.8	18	45.7	39	99.1
1¾	44	4.4	19	48.3	40	101.6
2	51	5.1	20	50.8	41	104.1
2½	64	6.4	21	53.3	42	106.7
3	76	7.6	22	55.9	43	109.2
3½	89	8.9	23	58.4	44	111.8
4	102	10.2	24	61.0	45	114.3
4½	114	11.4	25	63.5	46	116.8
5	127	12.7	26	66.0	47	119.4
6	152	15.2	27	68.6	48	121.9
7	178	17.8	28	71.1	49	124.5
8	203	20.3	29	73.7	50	127.0

yards to meters

yards	meters	yards	meters	yards	meters	yards	meters	yards	meters
1/8	0.11	2⅛	1.94	4⅛	3.77	6⅛	5.60	8⅛	7.43
1/4	0.23	2¼	2.06	4¼	3.89	6¼	5.72	8¼	7.54
3/8	0.34	2⅜	2.17	4⅜	4.00	6⅜	5.83	8⅜	7.66
1/2	0.46	2½	2.29	4½	4.11	6½	5.94	8½	7.77
5/8	0.57	2⅝	2.40	4⅝	4.23	6⅝	6.06	8⅝	7.89
3/4	0.69	2¾	2.51	4¾	4.34	6¾	6.17	8¾	8.00
7/8	0.80	2⅞	2.63	4⅞	4.46	6⅞	6.29	8⅞	8.12
1	0.91	3	2.74	5	4.57	7	6.40	9	8.23
1⅛	1.03	3⅛	2.86	5⅛	4.69	7⅛	6.52	9⅛	8.34
1¼	1.14	3¼	2.97	5¼	4.80	7¼	6.63	9¼	8.46
1⅜	1.26	3⅜	3.09	5⅜	4.91	7⅜	6.74	9⅜	8.57
1½	1.37	3½	3.20	5½	5.03	7½	6.86	9½	8.69
1⅝	1.49	3⅝	3.31	5⅝	5.14	7⅝	6.97	9⅝	8.80
1¾	1.60	3¾	3.43	5¾	5.26	7¾	7.09	9¾	8.92
1⅞	1.71	3⅞	3.54	5⅞	5.37	7⅞	7.20	9⅞	9.03
2	1.83	4	3.66	6	5.49	8	7.32	10	9.14

Index